T0221823

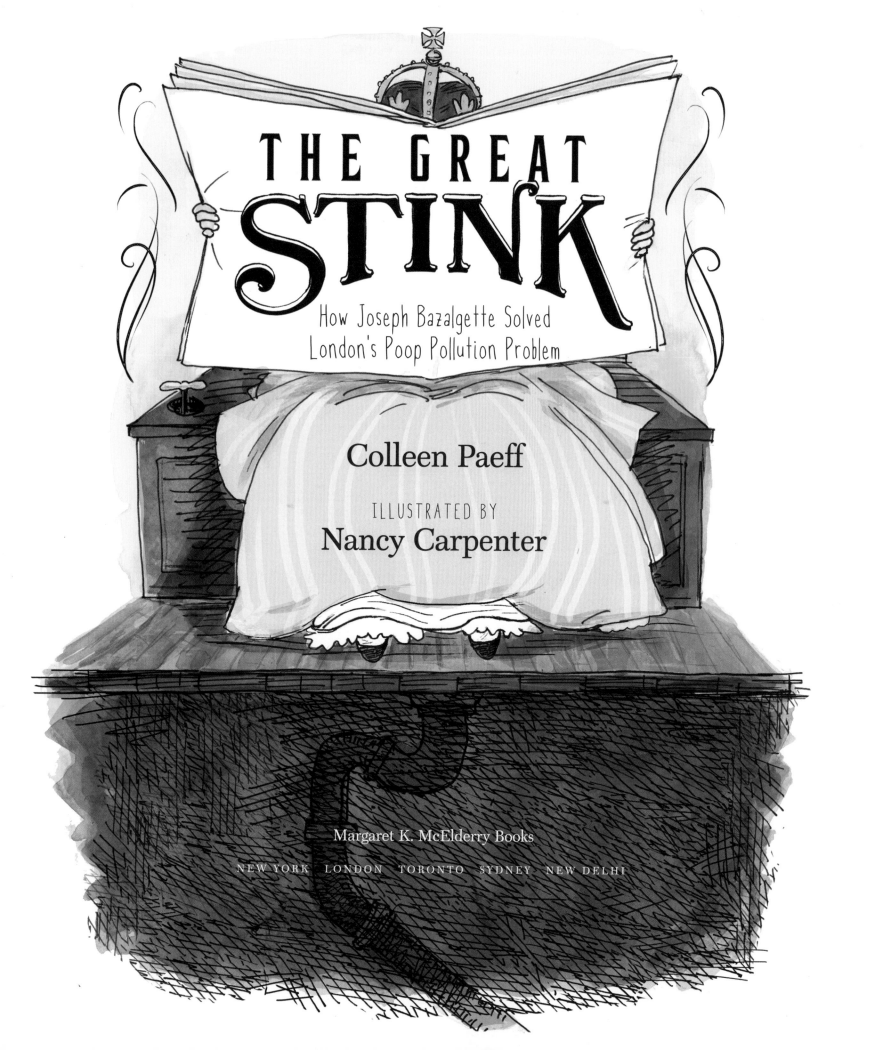

THE GREAT STINK

How Joseph Bazalgette Solved
London's Poop Pollution Problem

Colleen Paeff

ILLUSTRATED BY
Nancy Carpenter

Margaret K. McElderry Books

NEW YORK   LONDON   TORONTO   SYDNEY   NEW DELHI

NO MATTER HOW YOU DESCRIBE IT—

smelly, foul, fetid, rank, putrid, bad, or reeking—in the summer of 1858, London's River Thames STANK. What created such a revolting smell? No matter what you call it—feces, stool, discharge, dung, number two, or excrement—the answer is gross. The river was full of poop.

To find out why the world's largest city had a poop-filled river snaking through its center, and to discover who cleaned it up, we'll need to go back in time to a very different London.

1500

The problem starts with sewers. In London at this time, the sewers have one job and it has nothing to do with poop. They carry rainwater to rivers, so the city won't flood. It's not even legal to dump human waste into sewers. Instead, poop and pee go into deep holes dug in basements or backyards called *cesspools*.

Pee seeps into the ground, while poop piles up and up and up. A full cesspool means more than a smelly basement. It means it's time to hire the nightsoil men. These men shovel "night soil" (a.k.a. poop) into buckets and sell it to farmers, who turn it into compost for crops.

This system works for hundreds of years. But
then London's population grows and grows. . . .

1819

More people. More buildings. More poo. Flush toilets are slowly catching on, but all that extra water creates a malodorous mess. The nightsoil men's prices are so high that Londoners look for other ways to get rid of human waste.

Some people connect their toilets and cesspools directly to the sewer— sending pee and poop straight to the river. London is developing a serious poop pollution problem. And there's no plan to fix it.

But there's a bright spot in all this muck. It's a baby boy named Joseph Bazalgette. He's small and his family worries he won't survive. But luckily for London, he does.

1832

Joseph turns thirteen this year. He's still small, but he's survived London's first epidemic of the dreaded disease cholera. 6,536 people aren't so lucky. Some of them die after a few days. Some only last a few hours. Everyone in London fears they will be next.

1848-49

Members of Parliament, the country's government, are determined to wipe out cholera. They believe it spreads through smelly pockets of air called *miasmas*, and they aim to rid the streets of stench by sending pee, poop, dead animals, horse dung, chemicals, and everything else stinking up the city directly to the river.

Parliament demands that all toilets be connected to the sewers. And the sewers, of course, will carry the waste straight to the same place where Londoners are dumping everything else—the waters of the Thames. Unfortunately, they are wrong about miasmas—very wrong. It's not bad air that spreads cholera.

It's bad water.

Even worse, some water companies sell the river's polluted water as drinking water, which continues to spread the disease. But most Londoners believe their water comes from a clean part of the river. So they let any visible gunk settle to the bottom of their glasses—and they drink.

In spite of the government's fight against foul odors, London suffers its second, and most devastating, cholera outbreak. 14,137 people are dead.

CHOLERA STRIKES AGAIN

Once again, Joseph Bazalgette has survived. He's now an engineer with dreams of making London a better, cleaner, healthier place to live. One of his jobs is to map London's sewers.

He discovers pipes of different sizes, different shapes, and different slopes in every district. He encounters rotting bricks, blocked pipes, and poor design. In short, Joseph learns that London's sewers are a disorganized, haphazard, higgledy-piggledy mess.

1853–54

Cholera is back., 10,738 people are dead.

A magazine writes, "Where are ye, ye civil engineers? Ye can remove mountains, bridge seas, and fill rivers . . . can ye not purify the Thames, and so render your own city habitable?"

One engineer believes he can. . . .

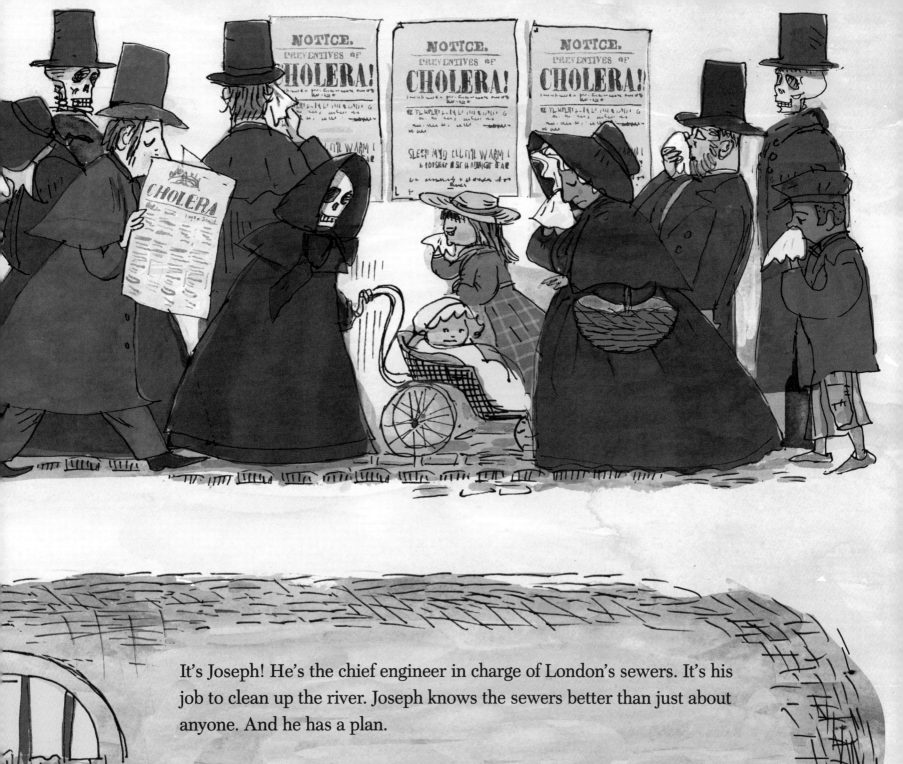

It's Joseph! He's the chief engineer in charge of London's sewers. It's his job to clean up the river. Joseph knows the sewers better than just about anyone. And he has a plan.

He wants to build new, gigantic sewer pipes along both sides of the Thames. They'll catch the sewage in central London, and gravity will carry it far from the crowded city where it will be pumped back into the water and the tides will pull it toward the ocean. Yes, at some point, the poop is going back into the Thames. Nearly everyone believes the doctors and scientists who say foul air, not water, causes cholera—even Joseph.

1856

Joseph submits his plan to the members of the Metropolitan Board of Works. They like it! The Board submits the plan to Sir Benjamin Hall. He must approve it before Joseph can start building—but Sir Benjamin doesn't approve. He thinks Joseph's plan releases the poop too close to the city.

Joseph starts again. He submits another plan containing longer pipes. But Sir Benjamin says longer sewer pipes are too expensive— Parliament won't pay. For two years, Joseph and the Board argue with Sir Benjamin and Parliament. How far away is far enough? Who is going to pay? Are Joseph's ideas best or should they hire someone else?

Meanwhile, every day there's enough poop flowing into the Thames to fill one hundred thirty-six Olympic-size swimming pools. And Joseph is powerless to stop it.

1858

Something is in the air. The people of London cover their noses with handkerchiefs. Members of Parliament run from their meeting rooms. Queen Victoria is practically poisoned. London is experiencing a heat wave. As the sweltering sun beats down on the rotting filth in the river, it creates a stench so putrescent, so feculent, so foul, Londoners give it a name—the "Great Stink."

People are terrified by the dreadful smell. They fear another cholera outbreak is coming. But Joseph is celebrating. The Great Stink has jolted Sir Benjamin and Parliament into action. Joeseph's plan for new sewers has been approved.

He can start building.

1859

Workers dig huge, open trenches in the streets.

1861

They tunnel beneath buildings, waterways, and train tracks — meeting in the middle with incredible accuracy.

1862

They even create new land. It's almost impossible for Joseph to find open space where he can build new sewer pipes without causing roadblocks, traffic, and major headaches for Londoners.

So in some areas he creates man-made riverbanks called *embankments*. To construct them, workers build long dams on both sides of the Thames, drain the water, and then build the biggest sewer pipes in the system right alongside the river. When the space is filled in, Joseph will use the new land to build roads, sidewalks, and parks where the people of London can enjoy clean air without poop-scented fumes wafting off the river.

April 4, 1865

Today is the grand opening of the southern portion of London's new sewer system. A band plays and flags wave as Joseph welcomes Prince Albert Edward (England's future king!) to the Crossness Pumping Station. Engineers, builders, clergymen, politicians, and other members of the royal family follow along as Joseph leads the prince into the engine house—an elegant building with a not-so-elegant purpose.

Inside, four enormous steam engines operate giant plungers that will pump London's sewage from far beneath the ground into a huge reservoir beside the Thames. At the right time of day—when the tide flows toward the ocean—the sewage will be released into the river.

There's no sewage in the underground reservoir today, though. Instead, it glows with the light of hundreds of colored oil lamps. Joseph shows off its vaulted ceiling, precise brickwork, and the heavy gate separating His Royal Highness from millions of gallons of poop. It's not exactly a royal palace, but Joseph's engineering feat is just as impressive.

Back aboveground he escorts the prince to one of the engines.

The prince pushes a lever. HISS. The flywheel grinds. CLUNK. The building vibrates. CHUG. HISS. CLUNK. CHUG. HISS. CLUNK. The engine roars to life. Joseph's southern sewer system is operational.

"Hooray!" Everyone cheers Joseph's great achievement.

1866

Cholera strikes again. 5,596 people are dead. But this time, they all live in the East End—an area not yet connected to Joseph's sewers. The rest of London is safe.

The evidence is too strong to ignore. Doctors and scientists gradually begin to accept that contaminated water—not air—causes cholera. By clearing the Thames of pollution, Joseph's sewers are saving lives.

1874

Welcome to Windsor Castle. The Great Stink is nothing but a smelly memory. The fear and anxiety that gripped Londoners from the street sweeper to Queen Victoria have dwindled. London's battle with cholera is over, and Joseph is being honored by the queen for his outstanding contribution to his country. He's gone from measuring and mapping pipes full of poop to knighthood—now he is *Sir* Joseph Bazalgette.

Newspapers have praised Sir Joseph's sewers as the most extensive and wonderful work of modern times. And in the years to come, historians will remember him as a "superb and far-sighted engineer" who "did more good and saved more lives" than any public official of his time. By cleaning the polluted river, Sir Joseph has made London a healthier, happier, better-smelling place to live. No matter how you describe that—stunning, neat, first-rate, grand, smashing, keen, or splendid—it's pretty great. And that doesn't stink.

POOP POLLUTION TODAY

No one can live without clean water. Humans, plants, animals—we all need it to survive. But as Earth's population grows and its climate changes, keeping our water clean becomes more difficult. When we think of water pollution, we often think of chemicals, oil, or pesticides. But did you know that sewage continues to pollute waterways around the world with dangerous results?

According to the World Health Organization, nearly two billion people get their drinking water from a source polluted by raw sewage, or sewage in its natural state.

They are some of the world's poorest people, and they live in areas without proper sanitation. In other words, they don't have safe ways to dispose of their poop. Every year, 3.4 million people die from water-related (which often means poop-related) diseases. Even today, people die of cholera, the same disease that killed so many in Joseph Bazalgette's era.

Thankfully, a group of more than fifty organizations involved in the fight against cholera have joined forces with an ambitious goal. They call themselves the Global Task Force on Cholera Control, and they plan to reduce deaths from the disease by 90 percent by the year 2030.

Many of the tools they need to make it happen already exist. Medication can save lives, and vaccinations can keep people from contracting cholera for up to three years. Access to safe drinking water, proper sanitation, and handwashing facilities can stop the disease before it starts. With trained aid workers, support from local governments, and funding from generous donors, the task force just might pull it off.

Though he didn't know it, Joseph used one of those tools to rid London of cholera. He provided the city with proper sanitation and safe drinking water by separating its sewage from its water supply. Nowadays, cities around the world go even further to prevent the spread of disease. They use wastewater treatment plants to kill disease-causing organisms in sewage. Then the treated sewage is safely disposed of or reused.

But even cities that treat their sewage struggle to keep raw sewage out of their waterways. In the United States, millions of people get sick every year from playing in or around water polluted by raw sewage. Raw sewage is one of the largest sources of pollution in Canadian rivers and oceans. And it's even polluting London's river Thames again.

The pollution usually occurs during heavy rain. Sewers that collect rainwater in addition to sewage get too full. Their treatment plants can't handle all the waste, and untreated sewage ends up in bodies of water used for drinking, swimming, or fishing.

Experts agree—it's time for an upgrade. Many cities are in the process of upgrading their sewer systems. In 2018 workers in London began the tunneling process for a super-sewer that will catch 94 percent of the city's overflow sewage before it gets to the Thames. But upgrades are expensive and can take decades to complete, so some cities are turning to "green infrastructure"—plants and trees—and letting nature lend a hand:

- Residents of the Puget Sound area of Washington State aim to plant twelve thousand rain gardens across the region. Bowl-shaped gardens that collect and absorb runoff from roads and roofs, rain gardens act like natural water treatment facilities. The plants' roots collect, absorb, and filter rainwater. Twelve thousand rain gardens could keep up to 160 million gallons of polluted water from entering Puget Sound each year.

- Ford's truck assembly plant in Dearborn, Michigan, boasts a 10.4-acre "living roof." It's completely covered with plants and grasses. The soil and plant roots keep millions of gallons of water from polluting Dearborn's river each year.

- The Lingang district of Shanghai, China, is becoming a "sponge city." The district is planting trees, building wetlands, creating absorbent roads, and installing green rooftops and rain gardens. Eventually, city leaders hope to prevent 70 percent of the city's storm-water runoff from flooding streets and polluting waterways.

Luckily, you don't have to wait for city leaders to prevent water pollution in your neighborhood:

- Build a rain garden: Plant a native garden designed to soak up rainwater runoff from pavement or rooftops.

- Plant trees: The roots of one mature tree can keep up to 4,600 gallons of water out of the sewer each year.

- Take a tour: Ask an adult to help you arrange a tour of a wastewater treatment plant near you and then . . .

- Spread the word: Talk to people about sewage. Tell them how it pollutes our waterways. And urge them to take action—just like you!

DETAILED TIMELINE

1500　Sixty thousand people live and poop in London.

Poop goes into cesspools, where it's collected by nightsoil men who turn it into compost for crops. Sewers, which go straight to the Thames, are for rainwater only.

The Thames supports abundant wildlife, including salmon, a sign of clean water.

1531　The Bill of Sewers, London's first major attempt to regulate its sewers, is passed. It divides London into eight districts. Each one is allowed to adopt its own rules about size, shape, and slope of sewers.

1596　The first flush toilet is installed at Richmond Palace for Queen Elizabeth I.

1810　One million people live and poop in London.

The rising prices of nightsoil men lead people to connect cesspools to sewers illegally.

1815　For the first time, it is legal to connect cesspools and house drains to sewers.

1819　Joseph Bazalgette is born on March 28.

1828　A Royal Commission inspects London's water supply and decides that drinking water should be drawn from sources other than the Thames. Some water companies ignore this advice.

1831–32 London's first cholera outbreak—6,536 people die.

Officials are convinced cholera is spread through miasmas, or foul-smelling air.

1834　Salmon can no longer survive in the polluted water of the Thames.

1836　Joseph begins his engineering career in Northern Ireland.

1842　Joseph opens an engineering practice in London.

1847　Joseph becomes sick from overwork and leaves London to recover in the countryside.

1848　Connecting house drains and cesspools to sewers becomes mandatory.

1848–49 London's second cholera outbreak—14,137 people die.

The Metropolitan Sewers Commission is established, combining seven of the eight districts created by the Bill of Sewers into one body.

1849　Joseph returns to London and works as assistant surveyor to the Metropolitan Sewers Commission, mapping the existing sewers.

1850　More than two million people live and poop in London.

Punch magazine publishes an illustration of an imagined drop of water from the Thames under the microscope. It's full of tiny little monsters.

1851　At the Great Exhibition in Hyde Park, 827,000 people use a flush toilet for the first time. More people install them in their homes, connected to cesspools. Cesspool flooding, already a problem, becomes worse.

1852　Joseph becomes Engineer to the Commissioners of the Metropolitan Sewers Commission, the top engineer in charge of London's sewers.

1853　London's third cholera outbreak—10,738 people die.

The Committee for Scientific Inquiries rejects the theory, submitted by Dr. John Snow, that cholera is spread through contaminated water.

1855　Metropolitan Board of Works is created to replace the Metropolitan Sewers Commission.

Scientist Michael Faraday tests the waters of the Thames and declares the river "a fermenting sewer."

1856　Joseph is appointed chief engineer of the Metropolitan Board of Works.

In June, Joseph submits his plan for London's new sewer system, but it is rejected.

For the next two years Joseph will revise and resubmit plans to cleanse the Thames.

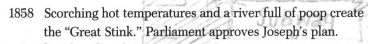

1858	Scorching hot temperatures and a river full of poop create the "Great Stink." Parliament approves Joseph's plan.
1859	Work on the new sewers begins.
1865	The Crossness Pumping Station opens, connecting the southern part of London to the new sewer system.
1866	London's fourth (and final) cholera outbreak—5,596 people die. All the cholera victims live in London's East End, an area not yet connected to Joseph's sewer. Dr. John Snow's theory that cholera is a water-borne disease starts to become accepted.
1868	Abbey Mills Pumping Station opens, connecting the northern part of London to the new sewers.
1870	A grand opening ceremony for the Victoria Embankment is held on July 13.
1874	Joseph Bazalgette is knighted.
1884	Joseph becomes president of the Institution of Civil Engineers.
1887	Sewage is no longer dumped into the Thames. Instead, it is transported out to sea on barges and dumped.
1889	Sir Joseph Bazalgette retires.
1891	Sir Joseph Bazalgette dies.
1998	Practice of dumping sewage at sea ends. Waste is incinerated, then safely disposed of or reused.
2018	Nearly nine million people live and poop in London. Joseph's sewers are in excellent structural condition and remain in use. Tunneling begins for a super-sewer, designed to catch overflow sewage from London's growing population before it pollutes the Thames.

AUTHOR'S NOTE

I never imagined I would write a book about poop. But then, as I was preparing for a trip to London, I stumbled upon three captivating words: the *"Great Stink."* I soon discovered it was one of the most disgusting and fascinating stories I had *never* heard.

My first day in London, I set out for the Crossness Pumping Station—the very place where England's future king started Joseph Bazalgette's southern sewer system. The engine house provided shelter for four huge rotative beam engines. There was a beautiful cast-iron arcade at its center. But what was most impressive were the engines themselves. Each main beam was the size of a school bus. Long connecting rods attached the main beam to a giant flywheel. When the flywheel turned, the beams would move up and down, pumping London's sewage from far below the ground into a vast reservoir. These engines haven't pumped sewage since the 1950s, but one of them has been restored and is occasionally turned on for visitors. I hope to see it in action someday.

FURTHER READING

Clean Water (Sally Ride Science, 2009) by Beth Geiger

How the Toilet Changed History (Essential Library, 2016) by Laura Perdew

Make a Splash! A Kid's Guide to Protecting Our Oceans, Lakes, Rivers, & Wetlands (Free Spirit Publishing, 2013) by Cathryn Berger Kaye and Philippe Cousteau

Poop Happened!: A History of the World from the Bottom Up (2010, Walker & Company) by Sarah Albee, illustrated by Robert Leighton

Poop Is Power (Rourke Educational Media, 2016) by Robin Koontz

You Wouldn't Want to Live Without Clean Water! (Franklin Watts, 2014) by Roger Canavan, illustrated by David Antram

You Wouldn't Want to Live Without Poop! (Franklin Watts, 2016) by Alex Woolf, illustrated by David Antram

SELECTED BIBLIOGRAPHY

Albee, Sarah. *Poop Happened!: A History of the World from the Bottom Up.* New York: Walker & Company, 2010.

Dobraszczyk, Paul. *London's Sewers.* Oxford: Shire Publications, 2014.

Frey, Holly, and Tracy V. Wilson. "The Great Stink of 1858." *Stuff You Missed in History Class.* How Stuff Works, January 14, 2013, 31:00. Accessed May 3, 2017. http://www.missedinhistory.com/podcasts/the-great-stink-of-1858.htm

George, Rose. *The Big Necessity: The Unmentionable World of Human Waste and Why It Matters.* New York: Picador, 2014.

Halliday, Stephen. *The Great Stink of London: Sir Joseph Bazalgette and the Cleansing of the Victorian Metropolis.* Stroud, UK: History, 1999.

Institution of Civil Engineers. *Sir Joseph Bazalgette: Civil Engineering in the Victorian City.* London: Thomas Telford, 1991.

Jackson, Lee. *Dirty Old London: The Victorian Fight Against Filth.* New Haven: Yale University Press, 2014.

Johnson, Steven. *The Ghost Map: The Story of London's Most Terrifying Epidemic—and How It Changed Science, Cities, and the Modern World.* London: Allen Lane, 2006.

Perdew, Laura. *How the Toilet Changed History.* Edina, MN: Essential Library, 2016.

Stebbing, Phil, dir. "The Great Stink." 2002; J. Basset, YouTube, February 15, 2014, 57:54. Accessed May 30, 2017. https://www.youtube.com/watch?v=MJWLJxiWgDY

ACKNOWLEDGMENTS

Several hundred Olympic-size swimming pools full of gratitude to the following people who helped bring this story to life:

Stephen Halliday, author of *The Great Stink of London: Sir Joseph Bazalgette and the Cleansing of the Victorian Metropolis,* generously answered my questions and reviewed my manuscript in advance of publication. Any remaining mistakes are mine alone. The volunteers and supporters of the Crossness Engines Trust made it possible for me, and others, to visit the Crossness Pumping Station—a true marvel of engineering. Kim Dewdney, London tourist guide with Discovering London, introduced me, live and in-person, to many of London's sewer-related sites. And Librarian for the Institution of Civil Engineers, Debra Francis, always managed to find obscure resources that answered tough questions.

Hi Sang Kim, operations and engineering manager at Hyperion Water Reclamation Plant, and Lisa MacAuley, wastewater treatment operator at Donald C. Tillman Water Reclamation Plant, provided me with an excellent education on the fascinating process of wastewater treatment. Aaron Clark of Stewardship Partners provided similar instruction on building rain gardens and the 12,000 Rain Gardens campaign.

Literary agent Clelia Gore expertly shepherded this manuscript from idea to sale, and Karen Wojtyla and her whole team at Simon & Schuster made it into a real book. My critique partners, Village Bakery writing buddies, and some very generous mentors provided feedback, friendship, and advice—and poop jokes. Finally, I couldn't have written this book without the unending support of the person to whom it is dedicated—my husband.

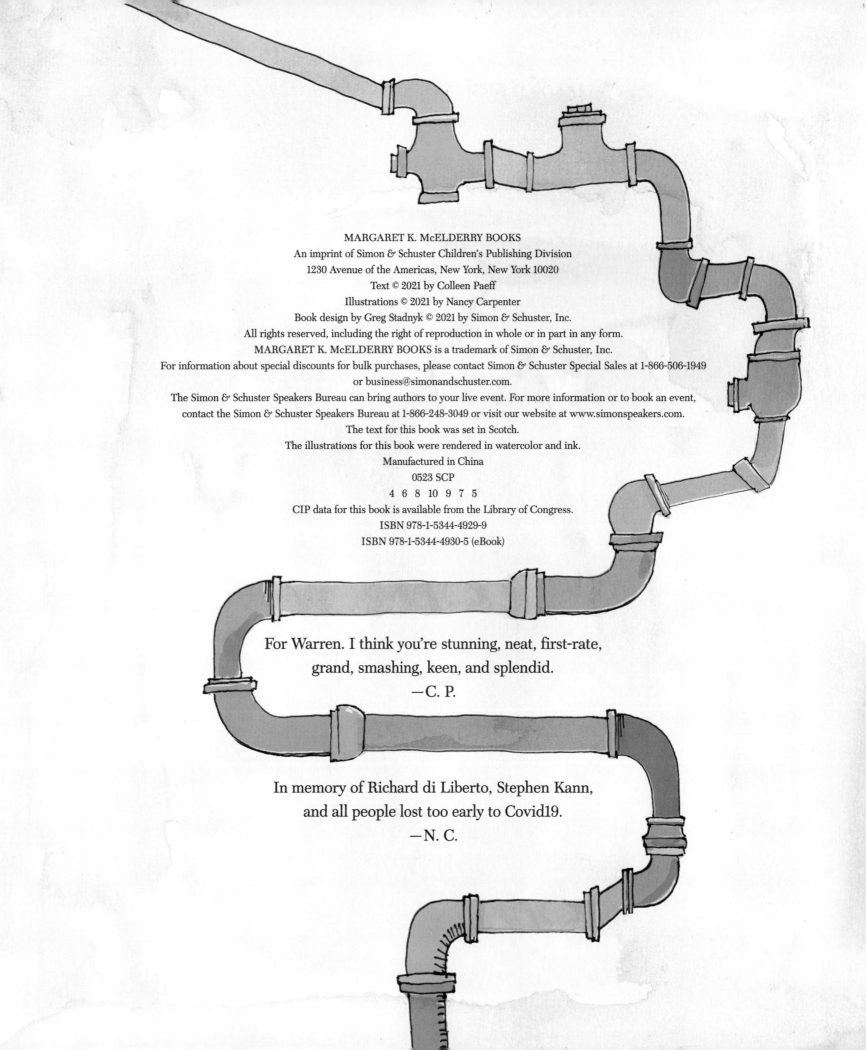

MARGARET K. McELDERRY BOOKS
An imprint of Simon & Schuster Children's Publishing Division
1230 Avenue of the Americas, New York, New York 10020
Text © 2021 by Colleen Paeff
Illustrations © 2021 by Nancy Carpenter
Book design by Greg Stadnyk © 2021 by Simon & Schuster, Inc.

All rights reserved, including the right of reproduction in whole or in part in any form.

MARGARET K. McELDERRY BOOKS is a trademark of Simon & Schuster, Inc.
For information about special discounts for bulk purchases, please contact Simon & Schuster Special Sales at 1-866-506-1949
or business@simonandschuster.com.
The Simon & Schuster Speakers Bureau can bring authors to your live event. For more information or to book an event,
contact the Simon & Schuster Speakers Bureau at 1-866-248-3049 or visit our website at www.simonspeakers.com.
The text for this book was set in Scotch.
The illustrations for this book were rendered in watercolor and ink.
Manufactured in China
0523 SCP
4 6 8 10 9 7 5
CIP data for this book is available from the Library of Congress.
ISBN 978-1-5344-4929-9
ISBN 978-1-5344-4930-5 (eBook)

For Warren. I think you're stunning, neat, first-rate,
grand, smashing, keen, and splendid.
—C. P.

In memory of Richard di Liberto, Stephen Kann,
and all people lost too early to Covid19.
—N. C.